L 81/9

ONCE THERE WERE DRAGONS

A BOOK
OF RIDDLES IN WORDS
AND PICTURES

JOHN MOLE
AND MARY NORMAN

ANDRE DEUTSCH

For Elizabeth, Henry and Tristram

First published 1979 by
André Deutsch Limited
105 Great Russell Street London WC1

Text copyright © 1979 by John Mole
Illustrations copyright © 1979 by Mary Norman
All rights reserved

Printed in Great Britain by
Fakenham Press Limited
Fakenham Norfolk

British Library Cataloguing in Publication Data

Mole, John
    Once there were dragons.
    1. Riddles – Juvenile literature
    I. Title   II. Norman, Mary
    793.7'35   PN6371.5

ISBN 0-233-97112-2

First published in the United States of America 1979

Library of Congress Number
79-64262

INTRODUCTION

All the poems in this book
Are riddles. Read one, and then look
Among the pictures for a clue –
They've been arranged to puzzle you,
So that to solve (say) Number One
You'll need to search, you'll have to thumb
Our pages till you find somewhere
The picture which completes the pair.
Be patient. Do not go too fast.
Save what's most difficult for last,
But if you end up really stuck
The answer's at the back. Good luck!

Grand and solo, polished brightly,
Dance of practised fingers nightly,
Claire de lunar or moonlightly.

Presto, forte, pathetique,
The world is mine because I speak
A language common yet unique.

I tax to brilliant extremes
Each maestro's formalistic dreams,
All variations and all themes.

Then, when his energy withdraws
To where you sit amazed, I pause
And share with him in the applause.

I am the shame beneath a carpet.
No one comes to sweep me off my feet.

Abandoned rooms and unread books collect me.
Sometimes I dance like particles of light.

My legions thicken on each window pane,
A gathering of dusk, perpetual gloom,

And when at last the house has fallen,
I am the cloud left hanging in the air.

Once there were dragons, with a pure flame,
And the burnt grass would always grow again.
No smoke, in those days, without a wholesome fire
Whether from good feasting or a funeral pyre.

Now there is nothing like that at all;
Man dreamed of money and he built me tall.
'More matter!' I cry, 'More matter, less art!'
And the stained plume at my tip gladdens no one's heart.

I lie at your feet
As if you'd wept me;

Looking down, you find
My blank face staring back

Or yours, perhaps,
A wobbly junket

Like the moon reflected
In some larger lake.

We rise, we fall,
Our corporation's global,
Cut-and-thrust executives
From Neptune Inc.

The world admires
Our liquid assets
And the fierce persuasion
Of our fluent tongues.

We overreach each other
In perpetual hurry;
Time is our essence
As the stock piles high

Then, past the rocks,
Our empire crashes
At the conference table
Of a polished beach.

Pity my silence pressing at your window
Frail and motionless against the night;
A baffled spectre framed by blackness,
Little moonflake, prisoner of glass.
This is my journey's end, receive me.
Brilliant keeper, rise and let me in.

Then later, when from a drawer perhaps
You take my body, wasted, brittle
As a shred of antique parchment, hold it
Gently up to the light I loved
But which bewildered me, until
I fly away again, a ghostly powder
Blown or shaken from your hand.

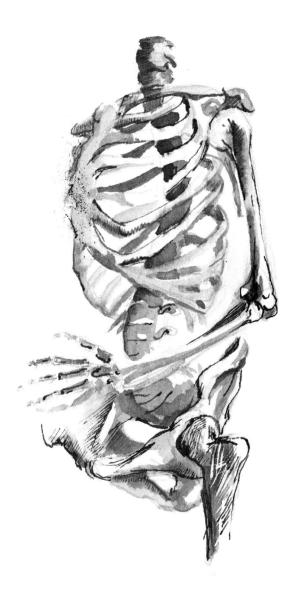

'Keep out' we say.
'It's Private, all of it,
So go away.'

'Beware' we bark.
'Our dog is lethal
After dark!'

'Danger!' we cry.
'Be sensible. You cannot
Want to die.'

But when you do,
Our lord, the pearly one,
May let you through.

I am unnumbered rooms to explore
Or a house of correction with X on its door.

Behold the temple of place and time!
Give something a name, and it is mine.

I am the only book on your shelf
Which never quite keeps up with itself,

But if you have my revised edition
I'm *almost* the total of definition.

Snow-motion, lumbering
Avalanche of fur,
From my wide glass kingdom
They brought me here

To your narrow world
Where the sky is grey
And white clouds are baffled
By each gloomy day.

I am the dead weight on your shoulders,
I am the vacancy behind your eyes,
I am the fear as you grow older,
I am the folly of the wise,
I am the headpiece, nodding, nodding,
I am the carapace of dreams,
I am the husk whose fruit's forgotten,
I am the fact and what it means.

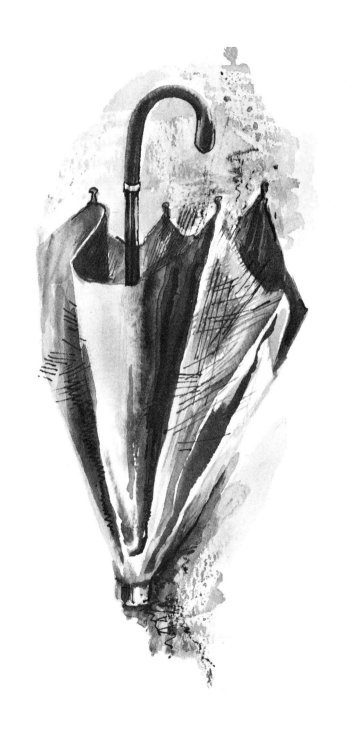

You should be glad that through the dark
I kept awake; instead
With something like a grunt or bark
You bash me on the head;

Which only goes to show, I'd say,
As sure as I'm wound tight,
That people often break by day
The vows they made last night.

Reveille. Dawn
Shakes out its music
On the battlefield.

We muster our thin forces
Slowly, slowly
As the shadows fall.

Touchdown. Wings
Announce the enemy,
Their fleetest air-arm.

Shrilling bayonets
Invade our trenches, and
The tug of war begins in earnest.

In the beginning
I became a wheel
And held enchantment
In my magic circles.

Then I became
The shape of order:
Spellbound citizens
Began to dream –

They dreamt their cities,
Pavements, statues;
Often I found my place
In one of those.

Paper may wrap me
But I blunt your scissors.
Heartless, my heart
Breaks many others.

Bag of bones,
Old bony,
Who'd be you
For love or money?
Yet for neither love
Nor money,
You'll be mine,
My Bony.

Whenever your meat's tough we tear it,
Whenever you're silent we're dumb,
And if we're a long pointed pair it
Could be that Dracula's come.

Whenever you grin we must bear it,
Whenever you're downcast we're glum,
And if you've a brace we must wear it;
We're a mouthful to live with, by gum!

Post-haste or slow,
Let there be no doubt
That wherever you go
I shall find you out
At whatever address,
And I mean business.

I'm dull, brown,
And I come at a price;
I watch you frown
With fear or surprise
At a name you know
Through my little window.

To send me again
Don't tear, use a knife
And a different name –
Ah well, it's a life!
Back and forth, back and forth
All over the earth.

Wrapped in a cloak,
I flash my silver lining;

Cheer up, now,
It's not as bad as that.

I may be dense,
I may be woolly-minded,

But you'll think more clearly
When I'm swept away.

Face to face or on the sly
I catch you with my sudden eye
And cannot, so they tell me, lie.

But when I let you reappear
Exactly as you were, oh dear,
The things you say, the things I hear:

'That's awful, that is really bad.
Do I always look so sad?
A cheat, a frame-up! I've been had.'

Oh thinning hair, oh broken tooth;
No one can give you back your youth.
How inconvenient the truth.

40

Flashing upon his
Inward eye – that did it!
Now we're rooted in comparisons
And blossom in a bliss
Of solitude. In fact

We've hardly seemed ourselves
At all since William
Mistook our ancestors
For poetry, and poetry
(Alas) for them.

The Roman built me straight,
They knew where they were going.
I am the quickest route there is
Unless the flies are crowing.

They say, when I lead to hell,
That I'm paved with good intentions.
I have known four strong legs give way
To fast four-wheeled inventions.

I'm what your cheery friend
Says 'Come on, let's have one' for;
And, I'm afraid, if your luck's running out,
When you reach my end you're done for.

Make-shift in Caesar's tent, I bore the weight
Of continents spreadeagled for his taking.

Courtly tales were told about my virtuous knights
But no one's perfect, and their King died broken-hearted.

Alexander, Charlemagne, a league of nations –
To and fro across me; treaties, bargains . . .

Empires pass; I watch them rise and fall,
A meeting of the board then liquidation.

As for you, you take your elbows off me.
Learn good manners and respect great men.

Who, sir, am I?
For a start, I hate sunshine
And deserve the penalty –
To be swallowed with good wine.
Miserable slitherer,
Landlubberly crustacean;
The French eat me, sir.
They are a wise nation!

The nastier the day
The nicer we are to know;
We're a kind, you might say,
Of aerial raincoat
Or a rooftop on the go
Or even, stretching it,
The back of a duck.

Some of us will almost fit
Your pocket. Others
Can bring bad luck.

Whatever the time and place,
We're an open or shut case.

Thick-set, accomplice of mortality,
I tell you secrets in a broken tongue

About yourself, about the stony-hearted
·Riddle that my words become.

Children used to give us to their teacher,
Rosy baubles shining on her desk,
And still, some say, we keep away the doctor –
Hardly Science, but how picturesque.

A famous novelist used to speak
Of a lady he met one day;
'How can I tell' she remarked 'what I think
Till I see what I say?'
Well, let my clattering keys unlock
The profusion of thoughts in your head
And, though it isn't a famous book,
You'll have seen what *you* said.

I am an elephant, I am a castle.
Come on inside and wet your whistle.

I am a coach complete with horses
Offering snacks or several courses.

I am a lion, red and white,

Who should be asleep by eleven at night.

I'm a jolly sailor, a poor king's head.
If you haven't guessed yet, have a drink instead.

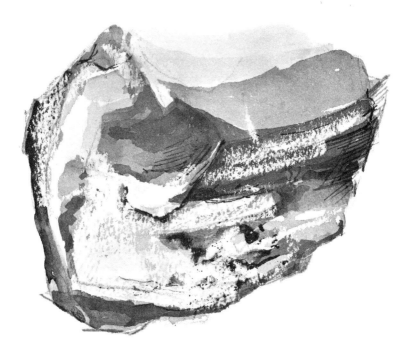

Built between man and man
By man, I bear his slogans:
Out! Vote Now! Go Home!
Poor dreamer,
Banging his head against me.

Through a bright autumnal air
We fall from grace, and from
The arms that held us.

The brilliant discourse of our veins
Has ended now; our fresh green thoughts
Must gossip with the dead ideas
Of yesterday.

Strewn, we lie at your feet
And when disturbed by shuffling children
Know that even they shall not escape.

There's a welcome at our parting
When we leave your new day starting.

When, at night, run out your time is
We are another word for Finis.

ACKNOWLEDGEMENTS

Dust and *Piano* have appeared in *All Sorts of Poems*
published by Angus and Robertson,
and *Moth*, *Skull*, *Stone* and *Waves* in *Thames Poetry*.